First English edition published by Editions Minerva S.A., Genève and Productions Liber
S.A., Fribourg
© MCMLXXVI by Editions Minerva S.A., Genève and
© MCMLXXX by Productions Liber S.A., Fribourg
All rights reserved
Library of Congress Catalog
Card Number : F128-18 - P27 1979 917 - 47'1'044 79 - 9793
ISBN : 0-517-28281-X
This edition is published by Crescent Books, a division of Crown Publishers, Inc.
a b c d e f g h
Printed in Italy

NEW YORK

Text by
Thomas Page

Crescent Books

New York

If, as Charles deGaulle once said, America is nothing more than the daughter of Europe, then New York City is the midwife. Simultaneously the most American and European of American cities, its birth, like that of America itself, is a result of the great vision that gripped western civilization in the Middle Ages: the search for a northwest sea passage to the fabled wealth of China and India so long cut off by the barricade of the Moslem Empire.

In 1524, Giovanni da Verrazano, an Italian working for the French king, sailed into the islands comprising New York Harbor and became fascinated by the red men who wore bird feathers on their bodies. Da Verrazano claimed all of North America as New France, a claim lasting no longer than the sudden storm that nearly sank his ship on the way out of the bay.

Months later, Esteban Gomes, a Portuguese in the employ of the Spanish king, sailed into New York Harbor during the dead of winter and right back out again as fast as he could. Manhattan Island was a frozen wind-swept waste, abandoned even by the Indians during winter.

Finally, in 1609, Henry Hudson, an Englishman working for the Dutch—even the explorers were cosmopolitan in those days—worked his way along the deep river on Manhattan's West Side that bears his name today. Believing India to be around each bend of the river, Henry Hudson sailed the *Half Moon* as far as Albany before giving up in bitter disappointment. A year later, the explorer vanished somewhere on the shores of Canada's Hudson Bay after mutinous sailors abandoned him and several shipmates on its arctic shore.

If there were any logic to history, New York would have been an English settlement from the very beginning, as was the rest of the East Coast, from Virginia to New England. The English Puritans had been heading for Manhattan Island when a navigational error turned them off course up to the rocky shores of Massachusetts.

Instead, it was a Dutch colony founded by the Dutch West India Company that purchased Manhattan from the Indians living on the north tip of the island, where Harlem now stands. Although a small tribe, the Indians claimed Manhattan's entire twenty-two mile length. The Dutch were forced to pay the exorbitant sum of sixty guilders—about twenty-four dollars—before they could build the town of New Amsterdam on the southern end of the island. The fortified north wall of this little town was to be known hundreds of years later as Wall Street.

North of Wall Street, Manhattan Island was lush green farmland laced with canals and lakes. Dutch peasant farms—called *boweries*—raised fine crops of beans, barley and buckwheat. Across the treacherous East River, farms and peach orchards covered the land, known as Breuckelen, "Broken Land" in Dutch, later to be known as Brooklyn.

Unlike the settlers of New England, who came here to escape religious conflicts, or those of Virginia and the Carolinas who came to extend the glory of their mother country, the Dutch envisioned Manhattan strictly as a commercial venture. The last Director General of the Dutch West India Company in New York was a man, with a violent temper and wooden leg, named Peter Stuyvesant, who had his hands full trying to run New Amsterdam. During his tenure, Holland and England were at war and the colony was hemmed in by over a hundred thousand English settlers as well as numerous Indians of uncertain disposition.

Trying to get Holland's aid in paying for the city's fortifications occupied much of Stuyvesant's time. It was a futile task, an early example of bureaucratic confusion that would be repeated time and time again throughout New York's history. Stuyvesant also seems to have spent an inordinate amount of effort keeping his colonists sober. Many of the enraged Directives that have survived complain about the enormous number of beer halls and taverns sprouting among the crowded wooden houses of the little colony. Similar problems would confront the later English Governors also. Francis Lovelace is remembered today as the man who knocked a hole in the courtroom of the old *Stadhuis*—City Hall—in order to get to the adjacent tavern and oil the wheels of justice with a little Jamaican rum.

The Dutch-English war came to the colonies in the person of James, Duke of York and Albany, brother of Charles II King of England. The King, in a fit of generosity, gave his brother all of the lands comprising most of New England and threw in New Amsterdam as well. When two of the Duke of York and Albany's warships sailed into New Amsterdam harbor on September 5, 1664, they were ready to take the city with the help of a few judiciously placed cannonballs.

Either because they knew their position was hopeless, or because their fort was ineffective against the English men-o'-war or simply because they were too drunk to die for the West India Company, the ten thousand Dutch of New Netherlands and New Amsterdam surrendered without firing a shot. Peter Stuyvesant informed his employers that the colony now belonged to the English, "Through God's will, thus unexpectedly."

The Director General washed his hands of politics and administration. He retired to his house and bowery where he spent the rest of his days working his land, praying in his private chapel and entertaining English governors from time to time.

The Peace of Breda formally ended the war in 1667. With what they thought was great cleverness, the Dutch formally gave up Manhattan Island and kept Surinam, in South America, believing it to be more valuable. Arguably, it was the greatest miscalculation in history, greater even than Napoleon's giving up the French territory of Louisiana for the paltry sum of twelve million dollars in the nineteenth century.

Although the cultural and intellectual origins of the American Revolution in 1776 were in Boston, Philadelphia and the towns of Virginia, it was New York City to which Lord Admiral Howe sent the bulk of his ships and a thirty-four thousand man expeditionary force, a large military undertaking for the eighteenth century, in an attempt to quell the independence movement. The city fell and in spite of the grand rhetoric and idealism of the Revolution, Washington's forces were chased all the way back to Pennsylvania.

New York endured seven years of military occupation. When the war ended, it was burnt and shattered but nominally the capital of the newly-formed United States of America. It was to remain the capital

At the southern tip of Manhattan, the Wall Street area seen from Battery Park. Following pages: two views of the same place, three centuries apart: midtown Manhattan seen from New Jersey.

for only six years.

On a summer night in 1789, Thomas Jefferson and Alexander Hamilton took a walk on the old Indian trail known as Broadway in front of George Washington's residence. The two men discussed the future of the country and decided, almost casually, that the capital should be located in Virginia close to Washington's Monticello home rather than in Brooklyn, Westchester or Harlem as had been suggested. A French architect was engaged to design a capital city from the ground up on the swampy banks of the Potomac river. Not surprisingly, it was named Washington.

Washington D. C. was only partially finished when the war of 1812 broke out. The British burned it down too. That was one war that New York City escaped without scars.

In 1969 there occurred a small footnote to history which in many ways is the most ironic of all to Americans and Europeans. A supertanker was fitted out with an icebreaking prow and sent off to realize the great dream that had brought the French, the Spanish, the Dutch and the rest of the Europeans to America in the first place.

The supertanker proceeded out of New York harbor up the east coast and into the Arctic archipelago, not far from where Henry Hudson met his mysterious end. After weeks of smashing through ice and gales, the supertanker emerged at the oil fields of the Alaskan North Slope. Beyond lay the open Pa-

cific and beyond that the shores of China and India.

Nearly five hundred years after Christopher Columbus, in an age of automobiles and airplanes, moon rockets and motorcycles, the supertanker finally found a northwest passage.

The name of the ship was the *Manhattan*.

Thus New York's history has a way of circling back to Europe.

In 1807, a writer named John Lambert had this to say about New York City: "All was life, bustle and activity. The people were scampering to trade with each other. Every thought, word, look and action of the multitudes seemed to be absorbed in commerce."

Modern New York is essentially a product of the nineteenth century. Its prominence stems from the fact that it is the world's greatest natural harbor. Although composed of five separate towns called boroughs—Manhattan, Queens, Brooklyn, Staten Island and The Bronx—its heart, soul and government reside in the towering skyscrapers and canyon streets of Manhattan.

Little physical evidence of the Dutch remains, but there are ample psychological traces. Many brownstone buildings of New York have raised stoops, a small stairway ascending to the first floor. The Dutch built these *stoeps* in New Amsterdam as a reminder of the broken dikes in Holland that sent sea water gushing over the land. Although the shores of Manhattan have never been flooded,

The twin towers of the World Trade Center, at the bottom end of Manhattan. At over 1,300 feet, they are the second tallest buildings in the United States, after the Sears Roebuck Building in Chicago.

Right: the plaza between the towers.

these stoops remained a feature of New York buildings well into the twentieth century. There are a few Dutch building foundations and, of course, place names such as Harlem, Flushing in Queens, the Bowery in Manhattan, Amsterdam Avenue, Stuyvesant Street and the like, but not much else. Since the early 1800s New York City has been a living organism that wounds and heals itself daily.

The city grew northward under the aegis of the English and Americans, inching its way slowly up Manhattan Island to the villages of Harlem, Yorkville and Bloomingdale. By 1800, it extended as far north as Canal Street and the farmland was getting crowded with country homes of the wealthier burghers. Just after the Civil War in mid-century, the New York Central railroad was electrified. The Hudson River railroad made stops at the villages of upper Manhattan and within years the city literally exploded over the remainder of the island, filling the scarce land so tightly that, eventually, the only place left to go was up into the soaring towers that characterize the city today.

"Overturn, Overturn, Overturn! is the maxim of New York!" wrote one appalled mayor in 1845. "The very bones of our ancestors are not . . . to lie quiet a quarter of a century and each generation of men seem studious to remove all relics of those which preceded them." New York builds and rebuilds itself hourly. New Yorkers are fond of saying it will be a great city if they ever finish it.

One of Thomas Jefferson's more grandiose plans was to end all foreign influence in the architectural look of America. The Federal style—basically nothing more than a gentler classicism—became what has been called our architectural Declaration of Independence. Had Jefferson lived to see what happened to New York in the nineteenth century, he would have been mortally embarrassed, for European styles invaded New York with a vengeance.

After the Civil War, it became fashionable for wealthy Americans to travel through Europe. Simultaneously, the first tidal wave of immigrants was crossing the Atlantic in the opposite direction, including some of the finest stonecutters, carpenters, and skilled laborers America has ever had. Until

On these two pages, a sampling of buildings, old and new, in downtown Manhattan.

Left and above: Wall St. in a festive mood, and at lunchtime.

The New York Stock Exchange.

then, Greek and Gothic had been the major fashions. After the war, the Americans were entranced by Venetian palaces, Second Empire façades, Beaux Arts, Romanticism, Victoriana, the result being that mansions and commercial establishments were dignified by everything European that could be duplicated. Crammed between the Hudson and East Rivers is two thousand years of European styles erected in less than two hundred. The architectural diversity is still astonishing today.

Historians saw the nineteenth and twentieth cen-

15

tury crowds of Central Europeans, Russians, Irish, Poles and other immigrants as a great social experiment, a "melting pot" of varied nationalities that would crystallize into a seamless whole. It did not quite work out that way. New York contains enclaves of separate cultures such as Chinatown and Little Italy whose inhabitants firmly retain their identity.

There is a church in Lower Manhattan called the Mariners' Temple founded in 1843 by Baptists for seamen. Shortly after its erection, the Mariners' Temple became the First Swedish Church. Then it was the First Italian Church, after which it was known respectively as the First Latvian Church, Norwegian-Danish Mission, First Russian Church and finally the First Chinese Church. Today its congregation is composed largely of Black and Spanish-speaking citizens, the latest of New York's major ethnic groups.

Perhaps on that night in 1789 when Jefferson and Hamilton were taking the night air on Broadway, they thought of New York City as too cosmopolitan, too diverse, too European to serve as the capital of a new Republic. Even though New Yorkers had rioted with patriotic fervor over the Stamp Act as did the rest of the colonies and even though the statue of George III, in Bowling Green Park (which still exists, incidentally), was pulled down and melted into musket balls three quarters of the city remained loyalist in sentiment to the British king. Perhaps Jefferson and Hamilton also recalled that it took a hundred years after Stuyvesant's surrender before preaching in English was begun in the city's Dutch Reform churches.

Perhaps Jefferson and Hamilton wondered on that night—as New Yorkers do today in their contemplative moments—exactly what New York City was. A seaport squashed into the southern perimeter of a small island? An artificial and therefore intensely human invention rising from water like a concrete Botticelli Venus—not as graceful perhaps, but every bit as seductive? An accident arising from fantasies about northwest passages and utopian societies, the gateway to a country that almost never existed?

Perhaps they thought it was just a dream all along

One of the imaginative murals which have brightened and/or rejuvenated many a dreary wall in Manhattan over the past few years. Above and below: two views of Fraunces Tavern, where George Washington delivered his farewell address before retiring from the political scene.

and did not really exist. Certainly no human imagination, not even Jefferson's, could have invented it as Washington D. C. was invented.

There are two types of thoroughfare in Manhattan. Avenues run north to south, streets from east to west. The spine of the city is Fifth Avenue, going from Washington Square all the way up to Harlem. Everything east of Fifth Avenue is called the East Side, everything west is the West Side.

Fourteenth Street in Lower Manhattan is a dividing line of history as well as geography. The heart of Manhattan's commercial and shopping district runs roughly north from Fourteenth Street to Fifty-Ninth where residential buildings begin to outnumber commercial ones.

Most of New York is laid out in regular grid-shaped blocks devised by nineteenth-century city planners, making it an exceptionally easy city to find one's way around in. Lower Manhattan below Fourteenth Street is an exception to this rule, and even native New Yorkers get lost among these narrow twisting streets, pathways and odd corners.

New York's financial district follows almost exactly the boundaries of old New Amsterdam. During the day, Wall Street, the Stock Exchanges, the office buildings and adjoining City Hall section are packed end to end with people. At night even these streets become silent. The bars and restaurants in Chinatown may remain open, ferries and ships still dock at the Battery and there may be a street festival uptown on Mulberry St., but down here, the closely packed buildings echo the rumble of the subway, the honk of faraway taxis and not much else.

Unless, of course, one's ears are sharp enough to detect the faint tap tap tap of Peter Stuyvesant's wooden leg as he checks the fortifications of New Amsterdam and wonders what is to become of his little colony.

Although the financial area is thoroughly modernized, nothing will ever widen its streets. Packed end to end with glass and steel skyscrapers among which are nestled many nineteenth century ones, this area presses against the shore of New York Bay. Since the seaport continues to be New York's major function, the financial district did not move northwards with the rest of the city.

Bowling Green Park was leased by the Dutch for one peppercorn and used as a cattle pasture before being converted into New Amsterdam's first park. The Beaux Arts-styled US Custom House, with its sculptured dolphins, rudders and columns, went up in 1907 on the site of the city's first fort, and George Washington's offices. This building sits on the oldest continually inhabited stretch of the city.

It is a pity, but Governor's Island, across the water, with its twin forts and Federal style Admiral's House, is not open to the general public. The island is where both the British and Dutch Governors lived—excepting Peter Stuyvesant who hated his quarters and moved to his farm. Governor's Island is regional Headquarter for the U.S. Coast Guard.

In spite of its critical placement in the United States, none of the forts of Manhattan ever fired a shot. Castle Clinton, resting in the green crescent expanse of Battery Park, was designed by New York's first native-born architect, John McComb. Changed to Castle Garden in 1823, its massive sandstone walls became a cultural center, devoted to musical concerts and occasional balloon flights. It was in Castle Garden that Jenny Lind, the Swedish nightingale, made her appearance in New York. The first great wave of immigrants, mostly Irish and German, were processed at Castle Clinton until that function was moved to Ellis Island. Stanford White, an architect whose name will figure prominently in this narrative, turned it into an aquarium and until 1941 it remained one of the most sensationally popular places in the city. It has been returned to its original form and designated a national monument.

Perhaps the most famous of the truly old buildings are Trinity Episcopal Church and Fraunces Tavern. Built in 1846, Trinity is a sharp pointed Gothic cathedral whose flowering churchyard contains the graves of Alexander Hamilton and of Robert Fulton, inventor of one of the earliest steamboats. The churchyard attracts many migrating birds who roost there, no doubt exhausted from maneuvering among the skyscrapers.

In Fraunces Tavern, Washington bade farewell to his troops, planning to resume his life in Virginia as

City Hall, and, above, the entrance to the Municipal Building. Top right: looking along Water Street.

a gentleman farmer. Fraunces Tavern is located at Broad and Pearl Streets and still serves food.

Six years after leaving New York, Washington was back again taking the oath of office with a borrowed Masonic Bible on Wall Street where the Federal Hall National Memorial now stands. The interior has been renovated and a museum installed.

Besides its association with two of the founders of the Methodist Church in America, the Italianate John Street Methodist Church (1841) proudly recalls a black slave named Peter Williams, who was purchased by the congregation, made a sexton and went on to make a fortune in the tobacco business.

The Morgan Guaranty Trust Building at 23 Wall Street is somewhat marred in its classical Greek elegance by shrapnel marks from the great Wall St. bomb blast of 1920, believed to have been the work of anarchists. This corner building faces the heart of Capitalism itself, the New York Stock Exchange, founded in 1792 under a buttonwood tree long since covered over in concrete and money. The Stock Exchange is open for guided tours. Some say the show on the Trading Floor is the equal of any musical, drama or comedy on Broadway.

Delmonico's restaurant on Beaver St. is one of the city's oldest, most elegant and—since their clientèle is mostly financial wizard—costliest. The James Watson house at 7 State Street is the only surviving mansion from the age of Washington's Presidency and is now a nunnery called the Shrine of Blessed Mother Elizabeth Seton, who was canonized recently.

Dominating the skyline of the financial area are the gigantic twin towers of the World Trade Center. Work still continues on these behemoths: landscaping a flowered plaza full of fountains and sculpture, planning more tours to the observation decks and similar projects.

Each morning the mayor of New York gets into his

The world-famous district known as Chinatown, truly a city within the city, as can be seen from these photographs.
At the top of this page: a glimpse of the Chinese New Year festivities.

limousine at Gracie Mansion on 88th Street and wends his way through traffic all the way downtown to lower Manhattan. Foley Square, City Hall and the municipal government buildings back imperceptibly into the financial district. Government buildings are almost always classical in design and New York's are no different. All of them were built between 1802 and 1914.

The first City Hall, the old Stadhuis, was recently uncovered by steamshovels clearing room for a stockbroker's skyscraper on Pearl Street. The one today at Broadway and Park Row is New York City's third and it was designed by a French-American partnership between John McComb and Joseph Mangin who combined Louis XVI classicism with American Federal. Based on the Hotel de Monaco of Paris and erected from 1808 to 1811, City Hall has received a veritable parade of kings, artists, soldiers

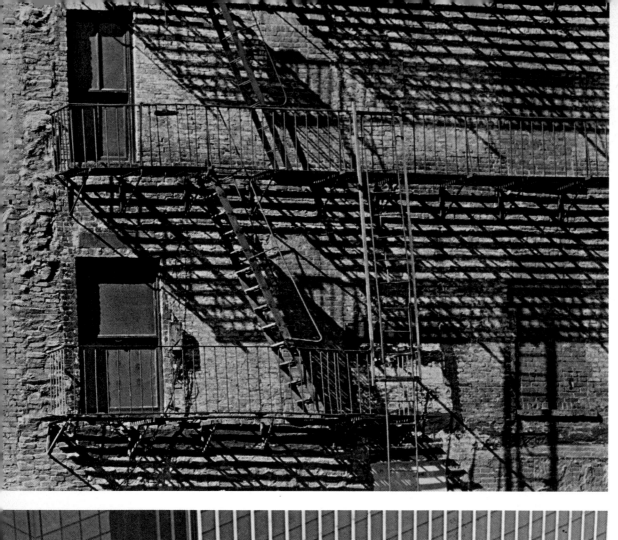

It is particularly refreshing to find, in the midst of so much concrete and steel, the occasional quiet tree-lined street (like this one, in Greenwich Village) which serves as a reminder of times past.

and citizens. Abraham Lincoln's body lay in state here while it was in New York.

City Hall Park's history is not so admirable. It has been a graveyard, public execution ground and the scene of numerous riots. The park is where the Declaration of Independence was read for the first time to New Yorkers. When told there had been a madhouse on the green in the eighteenth century, Mayor Lindsay commented that he was not surprised.

The 1912 New York County courthouse with its towering statues, columns and pediments is designed to hit the eye in as dramatic a way as possible. Its heroic proportions conceal the fact it is a simple hexagonal building modelled after a Roman temple.

The real eye-opener is Stanford White's 1914 Municipal building at Chambers and Centre Street, thirty-four massive stories of eclectic fairy-tale. Resembling a large Victorian bird with wings incompletely open, this exuberantly Roman concoction of towers, lanterns and urns floats on a forest of columns. The Municipal Building was built to complement City Hall. Instead, it very nearly swallows it up.

There is no man of whom New Yorkers are fonder than Stanford White. An architect of unquestionable genius living in an age of unquestionable excessiveness, Stanford White's life spanned the late nineteenth and early twentieth centuries, the gilded age, as Mark Twain called it, of high living, high corruption and high creativity.

Technically, Stanford White is classed as an eclectic who built Roman porticos here, Venetian palaces there, boiling down a melange of styles into witty, individualized, human-scaled buildings. His eclecticism matched New York's personality and his artistry graced it. Everybody in New York who lives in a building over fifty years old likes to think Stanford White designed it.

A taste of the days when the East River was a forest of masts and sails has been preserved at the South Street Seaport Museum. Moored at the docks are several old ships; The *Wavertree*, a full rigged merchantman, the *Caviare*, a Gloucester fishing vessel, the *Alexander Hamilton*, a Hudson River

In the middle of Greenwich Village, Washington Square: a favorite haunt of artists, both genuine and would-be, and also of non-conformists in general.

Fifth Avenue starts at Washington Square: the works of amateur painters are exhibited here several times a year.

Through the arch (bottom right), a glittering view along Fifth Avenue at night, towards the Empire State Building.

side-wheeler and the Ambrose Light ship. In spring and summer, jazz concerts and theater performances are held on the docks. The ships are open to the public, the breeze across the East River is fresh and the view of Brooklyn Heights is beautiful.

The Schermerhorn Row buildings are the oldest commercial ones in New York; they date back to 1811 and were built by a ships' chandler named Peter Schermerhorn. Sweet's restaurant on Fulton Street goes back to 1845 and still serves excellent seafood. The Fulton Fish Market gives a distinctive air—no pun intended—to the entire area. In the nineteenth century, it was considered stylish for the rich, the beautiful or the curious to gather with seamen and dock workers in the tight oyster bars and sample the best of the day's catch.

Dominating the entire seaport area is the greatest engineering achievement of the nineteenth century; the Brooklyn Bridge. Built by the father and son team of John and Washington Roebling, Prussian immigrants, the bridge was conceived as a symbol marking civilization's westward move from Europe to America and across the world.

By 1800 the city's commercial boundaries did not extend much farther north than Canal Street and the great bursting rush of population was still fifty years in the future.

The widest part of Manhattan lies in the area between Canal and Fourteenth Streets, and it has been over a hundred and fifty years since it was elegant. The Lower East Side is the part of Manhattan that bulges into the East River and it was the settling area for most of the arriving immigrants. Today this section of city blocks, punctured by Canal, Houston and

The United Nations Secretariat Building, on the East River, is one of the most famous features of the New York skyline.

Delancey streets, is crowded and raucous but still the most ethnically diverse area of New York City.

West Canal Street is surrounded by warehouses and traffic accessways to the highways and tunnels on the West Side, but central Canal Street has become one of the most wondrous assortments of discount, secondhand and flea market stores to be found anywhere. The sidewalks are lined with booths containing selections of everything from denim overalls to fire extinguishers to World War I gas masks. For reasons no one knows, much of Canal Street is devoted to assortments of unlikely, unusable and bizarre electrical equipment. Old transistors, used plexiglass, radio components, mountains of clothing, junked carburetors and artist's supplies pack the odd stores on both sides of cobblestoned Canalstreet. A few steps south of this street carries one directly into Chinatown, where the food is arguably the best for its price in New York.

One of the major ironies of Manhattan's northward march is that many of the old commercial buildings dating back through the nineteenth century—over ground once occupied by even older residential neighborhoods—are returning to residential use today. Oddly enough, New York was never considered a large-scale manufacturing center. The garment industry is the biggest enterprise of that type. Such manufacturing as there was in the city—metal-working, carpentry, etc.—was on a small scale, and was done largely in buildings such as those found in Soho.

Soho is a group of blocks running from Canal north to Houston (The word Soho comes from South of Houston) almost—but not quite—to Greenwich Village, which is slowly coming back to life after years of economic decline. The buildings of Soho are the only ones in the world with cast iron façades. Cast iron construction, the antecedent of skyscraper construction, became popular in the mid-nineteenth century when a passion for things Italian seized the citizens of New York. Cheaper and less time-consuming than ornamental stonecarving, cast-iron decoration could be stamped out in French Renaissance, Second Empire or neo-Greek in a matter of days, slapped over a storefront and maintained with

29

paint. Cast-iron building declined in the 1880s when steel-skeleton construction was perfected.

Soho underwent the cyclical changes that are New York's history. In the early days of independence it was a residential area, then after 1850, when Broadway had become a strip of stores, theaters and red light districts, Soho was abandoned. Today, because of zoning changes in the 1960s, Soho is one of the major creative centers of Manhattan. Attracted by low rents and cavernous warehouse spaces, artists, sculptors and film-makers are moving back into Soho and returning it to the residential status it had so long ago.

Perhaps the most famous of all New York's residential districts is Greenwich Village, located just below Fourteenth Street, both east and west. The Village has had a Bohemian reputation since the country estates and stables comprising it were broken up after the Revolution.

In the early 1800s, smallpox, cholera and yellow fever epidemics drove the panicky inhabitants of the city proper over their Canal Street boundary and into the village, where tent cities were set up among the estates. The tents evolved into small houses, until the village was so built up with permanent structures, by 1811, that it was impossible to impose the regular street pattern found above Fourteenth Street. But most important is the fact that the village remained residential by choice, successfully avoiding the commercialization that accompanied Manhattan's northward march as happened in Soho. Greenwich Village has always been Greenwich Village.

Nearly every style of architecture from the nineteenth century can be found in its compact area, including the narrowest house in New York, only nine and a half feet wide. Greenwich Village has been the home of countless artists and painters; Edgar Allen Poe lived here and Dylan Thomas socialized in the White Horse Tavern on Hudson Street. Mark Twain, John Barrymore, John Masefield, Walt Whitman and Henry James (born on Washington Square) all called the Village home at one time or another, living for a time in the flats, studios or small houses in the neighborhood.

One of the most innovative structures built in New York in recent years: the curved façade of the Grace Building on 42 nd Str. Right: view of a street at night.

The Jefferson Market Courthouse, an 1877 Victorian Gothic building at the junction of Sixth Avenue and Eighth Street, is considered the center of the Village's boutiques, pubs, jewelry stores and highly individualized restaurants which spill into the side streets.

East of Fifth Avenue below Fourteenth Street, New York City is unsure of what it is. The bookstalls of Fourth Avenue stand amidst another once-elegant section of the 1840's.

The Cooper Union Foundation Building on Cooper Square was endowed in 1853 by Peter Cooper, a steel and rolling mill industrialist, as one of America's first free colleges. It is here that Abraham Lincoln made the speech that launched him on a career leading to the Presidency. Besides its history as an educational institution, this enormous Italianate building used advanced steel construction that would make later skyscrapers possible as well as a round vertical shaft intended for a futuristic (by nineteenth century standards) machine called an elevator.

The Astor Library on Lafayette Street is an Italian palace with Victorian detail. It was the first library in America set up for use by the public.

Astor Place, a square close to the library, was the site of one the silliest riots in American history. A personal feud between an English and American actor over who was to play *Macbeth* in 1849 led to a bloody all-night explosion at the Astor Place Opera House during which police, outnumbered by thousands of howling, rock-throwing citizens, fired into the crowd killing twenty-two people (none of them critics so far as can be determined).

New York has a history of violent protest. The Macbeth riots cannot compare in scale to the Draft Riots of 1863 in which thousands of protestors, incited by Confederate agents nicknamed *copperheads*, rampaged throughout the city for four days in protest against conscription into the Union army.

Ironically the Astor Library now houses the Public Theater which saved it from demolition and reconverted its interior into modern stages. *Macbeth* has been performed there many times without incident and so has some of the boldest modern theater in

New York.

Fifth Avenue still remains modern New York's backbone. Time, taxes and the Great Depression of the 1930's ended its status as a residential preserve of the rich. Its northern sections blend the Upper East Side, where the neighborhoods are quietly opulent, and the Madison Avenue Art galleries, particularly the Whitney at Madison and Seventy-Fifth Street, which challenge the *Grande Dame* of New York museums, the Metropolitan Museum of Art. Fifth Avenue has preserved its past and placed it alongside the present. Its changing faces resemble the layers of time and urban development one might find laid out in an archaeologist's pit. From south to north a journey up this avenue is a journey from the turn of the century to the present day.

At Madison Square and Twenty-Third Street, Fifth Avenue joins Broadway in a large open area which was the most fashionable one in the city during the 1890s. The site of Stanford White's Madison Square Garden, this crossroads is dominated by what was the first skyscraper ever built; the Flatiron Building. Twenty stories tall, resembling the prow of a ship about to sail up the avenue, the Flatiron building was erected in 1902 when, in the words of R. Buckminster Fuller, "Architects were still pretending there was no such thing as steel." Since steel was a relatively new material to handle in quantity outside railroads and heavy industry, Fuller's dictum is right. The advanced steel skeleton frame with its wind bracing and great strength was hidden under a frosting of neo-Renaissance detail.

Curiosity about the Flatiron Building was not the only thing to bring crowds down to Madison Square after it was built. The builders had cleared ground for the foundations and this open space caused gusty winds to lift the skirts of women to a scandalous ankle height. It is said the problem of girl watching became so acute at Madison Square, extra police were employed just to keep the men moving.

North of Madison Square at Thirty-Fourth Street, where Altman's store still stands, the visitor will find himself at the foot of the Dean of Skyscrapers, the 102-story Empire State Building. It went up from 1929 to 1931, to great national excitement. The very

The amazing Flatiron Building, on Madison Avenue, at the corner of Broadway and Fifth Avenue; built in 1902, it was for many years the most revolutionary building in the world.

33

top, where a television antennae protrudes, was originally a moving mast for dirigibles until the *Hindenburg* crash burned mankind's dreams for this mode of travel. From the observation deck of the Empire State Building one can see a distance of fifty miles. One of the most striking of sights from this vantage point is the nearby Chrysler Building. At sunset, the top of the Chrysler glitters like diamonds. Diamonds are mixed in with the cobalt and tungsten steel comprising it. This steel was developed in Germany at the Krupp Works in 1928 and is reputed to be the hardest ever forged.

Two full blocks of Fifth Avenue, Forty-First and Forty-Second Street, are occupied by the New York Public library, a majestic Beaux Arts structure flanked by two stone lions. (The lions only roar when a virgin passes between them according to New Yorkers.) The largest library in America next to the Federal Library of Congress, the library was built in 1895 on the grounds where a reservoir once stood. Behind it is Bryant Park where office workers congregate during lunch hours for city-style picnics.

Fifth Avenue from Forty-Second to Fifty-Ninth Streets is largely devoted to what is called the luxury retail trade. Airline offices, jewelers, boutiques and fashion shops and bookstores are mixed in with the varied office buildings.

The New York subway: feared by some, extensively plastered with psychedelic inscriptions by others. "Functional" is definitely the word to describe this subway system. Following pages: downtown Manhattan.

led by the Mayor, is an affair dating back even before the major wave of immigrants arrived. In 1779, four hundred Irishmen celebrated their patron Saint at the Bowery. They formed a parade behind, of all things, a British Colonel trying to enlist them in the King's army to fight George Washington.

Rockefeller Center was under construction for eight years (1931–1939) and is sometimes called the Village Green of modern New York. A handsome block of buildings interwoven with fountains, walkways, statuary and a skating rink which is converted to an outdoor restaurant in warm weather, the Center is considered one of the most beautiful examples of urban design in the world. Originally the Center was to have been the home for a relocated Metropolitan Opera House but the stock market crash forced a change of plans. The neighborhood was occupied by rows of elegant brownstones converted into Prohibition "speakeasies,"—illegal saloons—so John D. Rockefeller Jr. razed them and built an urban complex of his own.

Rockefeller Center was the focus of a national uproar during the final stages of its construction. The Mexican artist Diego Rivera painted a mural fresco on the RCA Building wall depicting, among other shockers, Lenin's head amongst various Socialist figures marching behind tractors, working in factories, and other Marxist themes, all of particular appeal during the Depression. Beside a scene portraying armies of unemployed being beaten by police was a microscopic view of the world swarming with venereal disease germs. Considered inappropriate in a plaza named after the founder of the Standard Oil Company, the fresco was destroyed at midnight by a wrecking crew before a full scale riot could occur. It was replaced by one that includes a figure of Jesus Christ in its design.

The Museum of Modern Art is not exactly on Fifth Avenue. It is just off it on Fifty-Third Street and it is the best and most comprehensive museum of its type in the world. Besides Picasso's *Guernica,* works by Monet, Cézanne and others, a variety of films and exhibits, the Museum contains a sculpture garden and restaurants.

On the corner of Fifty Second and Fifth is a large

IT is appropriate that New York's largest monument to spiritual wealth, St. Patrick's Cathedral, faces New York's most striking monument to material wealth, Rockefeller Center, on opposite sides of Fifth Avenue. St. Patrick's took so long to build (1858–1879) that it spans the styles from American Gothic, in its general pointed massiveness, to Victorian Gothic in the details of its pinnacles and pediments. This mixture of styles with some French elements added in the Lady Chapel, built in 1906, make St. Patrick's the most comprehensive example of Gothic Church architecture in New York. Its being named after the patron Saint of Ireland indicates the pivotal role in American history played by the Irish immigrants, particularly those who fled the potato famine and came to America. The annual St. Patrick's Day parade down Fifth Avenue, traditionally

On the corner of 34th Street, stands New York's most famous building, the Empire State Building. This distinctive feature of the New York skyline is even more striking at night, when its top floors are floodlit in color. Following pages: the Chrysler Building, famous for its unusual pinnacle and an assortment of New York street scenes.

39

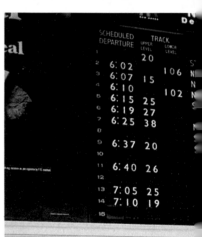

SCHEDULED DEPARTURE	TRACK UPPER LEVEL	LOWER LEVEL
6:02	20	
6:07	15	106
6:10		102
6:15	25	
6:19	27	
6:25	38	
6:37	20	
6:40	26	
7:05	25	
7:10	19	

Tickets

Italianate mansion belonging to Cartier's. How this house managed to become the property of the jeweler's is a curious example of shifting values over the last seventy years. Cartier's had supplied jewels to the French court since the eighteenth century. They became international when Edward VII purchased a set for Queen Alexandra thus attracting the interest of everybody from Indian rajahs to Americans. Cartier's opened a small shop in lower New York and decided to expand in 1917. Thinking the mansion of Morton Plant, an investment banker, would be ideal, with its small interior spaces, for the sale of small invaluable baubles, Cartier offered to trade a set of matched black and white pearls for it. Plant accepted and Cartier's moved in. The jewels had been estimated at a value of a million and a half dollars in 1917. They were revalued at a hundred and fifty thousand when Mrs. Plant died in 1956.

Crowning the junction of Fifth Avenue and Central Park South is the Plaza Hotel. Erected in 1908, in the age of Edward VII, with its conscious pursuit of elegance, this French Renaissance structure, with its turreted corners, balconies, balustrade and rich detail has figured in more plays, novels and stories than can be counted. Since it was built the Plaza has continued to be the scene of some of New York's most elaborate weddings, parties and social events.

At this point Fifth Avenue's character is formed decisively by the green acres of Central Park, over which the Plaza has an incomparable view. Fifth Avenue is lined with residences converted to other uses, such as apartment buildings and consulates, all facing the Park's eastern edge.

In 1859, while Thirty-Fourth Street was being developed, a Commission composed, among others, of William Cullen Bryant, a poet, and Washington Irving, a writer and essayist, became alarmed at the prospect of Manhattan's headlong growth. This Commission sponsored a nationwide design contest for parks which were to be implemented before the island was completely covered in concrete.

New York City is somewhat lacking in small neighborhood parks. In 1838 the City Surveyor's Of-

Views of Grand Central Station and Penn Station.

Top and right: two views of 42nd Street, the nature of which varies extensively as it crosses Manhattan island; some regard it as the boundary between Uptown and Downton. Above: another curved façade.

46

The bright lights, movie theaters and varied entertainments to be found on Broadway, at Times Square. Above: sudden weather changes are frequent in New York.

Above: the venerable Old-World-style premises of the Cartier jewelry business, on Fifth Avenue.

While Broadway, which runs from one end of Manhattan to the other, is one of the longest avenues in the world, Fifth Avenue is the most elegant: half-way along the avenue is St. Patrick's Cathedral (right).

Fifth Avenue is the scene of many of New York's traditional parades.
Right: Fifth Avenue and Rockefeller Center on a fine summer day.

fice prepared a plan for eighteen small parks in Manhattan to be built on land plots set aside for that sole purpose. The plans were never put into effect. Gramercy Park, between Twenty and Twenty-First Streets on the East Side, is a private preserve whose original owners were said to have gold keys to the fence surrounding it. Battery Park, City Hall Park,

Prospect Park in Brooklyn and a few others, as beautiful as they were, did not exist in sufficient numbers to allow the city to "breathe."

With Frederick Law Olmstead and Calvert Vaux's winning design for Central Park (originally named Greensward), the city made up for lost time. Begun in 1859 on eight hundred forty three acres of pesti-

Above: construction nearing completion, between Park Avenue and Fifth Avenue.

Above and following pages: the splendid *Rockefeller Center,* surrounding Rockefeller Plaza—one of the major New York tourist attractions.
Left: the statue of Atlas holding up the world, outside the International Building, at Rockefeller Center. Right: decorative work on the doors of the Center.

lential swampland inhabited only by thousands of squatters sharing their shantytown quarters with the mosquitoes, Central Park was finally completed twenty years later. The groves, ponds, glades, footpaths and zoo make it one of the supreme examples of advanced nineteenth century city planning.

Parks tend to grace the neighborhoods bordering them. Central Park South connects the square of the Plaza Hotel with Columbus Circle at Broadway, and is lined with many beautiful shops and apartments. Olmstead's original plans emphasized that the borders of the Park be left untouched but there are two spots where structures have been built on land set aside for them. One, the Metropolitan Museum of Art is actually on its own grounds.

Beyond question, the Metropolitan Museum of Art is the finest and most comprehensive in the United States. Nestling in the four block stretch of Fifth Avenue from 80th to 84th Streets, the museum contains fifteen separate units built over a century and still expanding with each acquisition. Although the "Met's" first unit, a Victorian Gothic building, faced Central Park, it is dwarfed by the Central Pavil-ion of neo-Classic and Beaux Arts columns and arches that turned its orientation to the Avenue.

The Metropolitan's art comes to it by bequest, gift or donation. Its most famous recent acquisitions are Nelson Rockefeller's unique primitive art collection and the Denderah Temple which was a gift by the Egyptian government. The Met has come a long way since 1870 when it began with 174 Dutch and French

A beauty perhaps not consciously planned by the architects: reflections of steel and glass. Above: Park Avenue approaching the ramp leading around Grand Central Station and under the Pan Am Building.

57

58

paintings on display in temporary quarters belonging to a Dance Academy.

All of the great private mansions along Upper Fifth Avenue were built between 1900 and 1930. Most have been converted to schools, charitable organizations or cooperative apartment buildings. The Frick Gallery on 1 East 70 Street, once the home of a steel executive, has been converted to an art museum, its Louis XIV style complemented by a formal French garden on 70th Street. The neo-classical James B. Duke house, also inspired by French design, now contains the Fine Arts Institute of New York University, within limestone walls so white and fine they appear to be marble. The R. Livingston Beekman house at 66th and 67th Streets, now the Yugoslavian Mission, compresses a sense of monumentality and scale into a mere cottage of a building only two windows wide.

On Fifth Avenue and 88th Street stands the Guggenheim Museum, the only building Frank Lloyd Wright ever designed *in toto* for New York and one of the most unique of all of his unique creations. Visitors to this cylindrical building, which is devoted to modern art, begin from the top and proceed down a spiral system of ramps to street level.

The Museum of the City of New York on 103rd and 104th Streets is the first in America to be devoted exclusively to the life of a single city. Housed in a neo-Georgian marble and brick building, the museum includes among its countless toys, costumes, dioramas and furniture, one of the finest collections of ship models to be found anywhere.

These Upper East Side neighborhoods are the Madison Square of today. Spilling down the side streets to the art galleries of Madison Avenue and the homes along Park Avenue are modest neighborhoods mixed with small restaurants and shops. North of the Museum of the City of New York, Fifth Avenue leads to Spanish Harlem. On a sunny weekend in spring, it becomes a magnet for strollers and lovers of odd, curio shops. The rest of New York's East Side developed in its own way.

In 1900, one seventh of New York's population was foreign-born. Horsecars and trolleys crammed the streets and Thomas Edison's new Electric Light

In the heart of the proudest part of the city, some patches of nature have been preserved: the trees of the one shown here are lit up in winter; in summer a refreshment stand is in operation.

Power Plant on Pearl Street had not replaced the green gas haloes that glowed over the city's streets at night.

Moving its population through the narrow streets at low cost and high efficiency was a problem that could be solved in two ways. Public transportation could go underground as it did in London in 1863 with the first subway or it could go upwards over the streets. Since Manhattan rests on solid rock, it was logical that Charles T. Harvey's elevated Patent Railway System first tested on Greenwich Street in 1867 would be approved by the city. Harvey's train was raised to a distance of thirty feet or more above street level and ran on steel braced tracks. Beginning in 1871 the "Els" were drawn by steam engines rather than cable. Eventually the tracks ran the length of Ninth Avenue, Sixth, Third and Second Avenues where they serviced the Lower East Side and crossed the river to Brooklyn.

The Els were a mixed blessing. True, they transported millions of people a day, tied Manhattan into some kind of mobile order that kept the streets as uncongested as possible and brought Harlem into the life of the city; but cinders, coal dust, steam and especially their shattering noise blasted the neighborhoods through which they passed. Third and Second Avenue were blighted so completely that these areas did not begin to recover until mid-twentieth-century, after most of them had been torn down. Even before World War Two, whole sections were dismantled, some of the scrap steel and locomotive parts being sold to Japan, incorporated into its war equipment and returned to America in the form of bombs and aircraft.

The Subway System was finally launched with Rothschild money in 1904. Two years before, New York State ordered the New York Central Railroad to electrify all its urban rails or leave the city.

The particular system that annoyed residents was a raw open gash running down Fourth Avenue to a terminal called Grand Central Station. Steam and smoke fouled the air in mid-town to an unbearable degree. With rare boldness the New York Central not only agreed to electrify its city lines, it rebuilt Grand Central Station into one of the most beautiful exam-

A few blocks from this virtually aerial view of Madison Avenue (above), the visitor is surprised to find a quiet (well, almost) square and also horse-drawn cabs!

ples of Beaux Arts architecture to be found anywhere. Crowned by the sculpted figures of Hercules, Mercury and Minerva, Grand Central went into operation in 1913 and within twenty years Fourth Avenue was renamed Park Avenue. The station's system of underground connecting ramps and transfers to Times Square were to serve as the model for the underground concourse at Rockefeller Center.

Most remarkable of all, the station converted Park Avenue into a combination commercial and residential boulevard, divided by trees, that rivals Fifth Avenue in its beauty. The wideness of the street, uncommon in New York, resulted in an architectural mix in which the old and very new exist side by side.

The very old is represented by an eclectic Byzantine church with a Provençal Romanesque porch called St. Bartholomew's on 50th to 51st Streets.

The East Side residential districts closer to the East River were rediscovered in the 1920s. The shoreline itself was not considered attractive because of the "Gas House District," an area of huge gas storage tanks that lined the river. Tudor City, an apartment and hotel complex, a growing number of hospitals and churches, Sutton Place, Beekman Place and East End Avenue all came into fashion then. Tudor City faces away from the United Nations for good reason; the land on which that august body of diplomats rests was a gigantic, smelly stockyard. Today this complex, with its thin green Secretariat Building, its sloping General Assembly Hall, its gardens and plazas, is one of the most familiar structures in the world. The presence of the UN spurred development all along the East Side avenues and streets.

In the 1960s along the lengths of First, Second and Third Avenues arose clusters of combination discotheque-Pub-restaurants nicknamed Singles bars. These raucous, exciting caves are the latest manifestation of New York's night life and a direct descendant of the speakeasies that lined the streets of the East and West Side.

Prohibition, as the world knows by now, was one of the most insane pieces of legislation ever passed by the Federal Government. By banning the sale of

Sixth Avenue is officially named the Avenue of the Americas: the heraldic devices of each of the States of the New World hang from lamp-posts along the avenue.

The vegetation, the lake and the paths of Central Park...

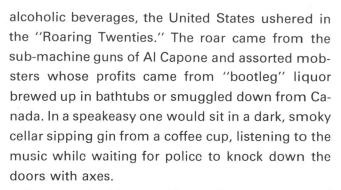

alcoholic beverages, the United States ushered in the "Roaring Twenties." The roar came from the sub-machine guns of Al Capone and assorted mobsters whose profits came from "bootleg" liquor brewed up in bathtubs or smuggled down from Canada. In a speakeasy one would sit in a dark, smoky cellar sipping gin from a coffee cup, listening to the music while waiting for police to knock down the doors with axes.

If cops and robbers had been all that came out of the Prohibition era, it would not rate mention in a book such as this. The fact is that something quite extraordinary did arise from New York City's experience with speakeasies, a new music with its roots hundreds of miles south in New Orleans and the bayou country. F. Scott Fitzgerald termed the 1920's, the "Jazz Age."

Jazz was a music peculiarly suited to the tight, densely crowded, hidden cellar or private club that was a speakeasy. Although it had been known for

New York has some of the most eminent shrines of world art, from the Metropolitan Museum and the venerable Carnegie Hall to the palatial cultural complex of Lincoln Center (right). Bottom right: a statue by Dubuffet, at Chase Manhattan Plaza.

years in the South, it was not until Paul Whiteman, a bandleader, gave a "jazz concert," and George Gershwin wrote "Rhapsody in Blue" that New York noticed it. Chicago and Kansas City both had clubs devoted to jazz but the jazz men, the composers, the singers, the trumpet players and trombonists poured north toward the rafters and ceilings of speakeasies from Harlem down Broadway to the Village, where they received a welcome loud enough to send this music over the world. Someone, some-

The unique and astonishing Guggenheim Museum and the sculpture garden of the Museum of Modern Art.

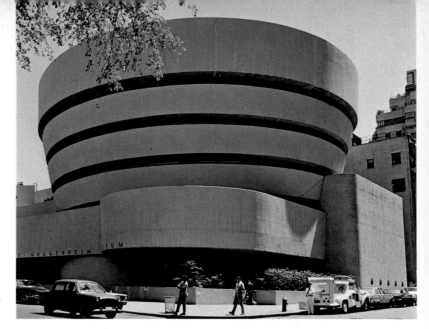

where in the 1920's gave New York City one of its enduring nicknames, the Big Apple. Big Apple is a jazz colloquialism meaning the place one goes if one wants to be successful. Consequently, along the west 50's and in spots in Harlem and the Village, jazz made its way to the ears of the world and ranks as one of the happier effects of Prohibition in Manhattan.

East Eighty-Sixth Street is called both Yorkville and Germantown. Settled by Germans anxious to leave the Lower East Side in 1900, this crosstown street is lined with beer halls, sausage shops and German restaurants.

Around the corner, where Eighty-Sixth Street runs into East End Avenue, is a line of small row houses in the Queen Anne style; called Henderson Place, it faces Carl Schurz Park.

During the Revolution, this peaceful Park was fort with a battery of artillery which was burned by the British. The handsome wooden Federal house at 88th Street, almost lost in the neighborhood, would be just another oddity except for one fact; it is the Mayor's residence.

Tradition has it that Gracie Mansion was designed by Major Charles L'Enfant, the French architect who made the master plan of Washington, D.C. The country villa of a Scottish merchant named Archibald Gracie, the house spent two hundred years under the ownership of various groups including the Museum of the City of New York, before being designated as the Mayor's residence in 1942.

Fiorello La Guardia was the first Mayor to live in it. A nephew of one of Garibaldi's men, the "Little Flower" was one of New York's most beloved Mayors. Besides initiating public housing projects, slum clearance and corruption drives, La Guardia used to read the comic strips aloud to children over the radio every Sunday. After the city decided to arrange a permanent residence for its Mayor, a succession of sites were offered, culminating in a seventy-five room marble chateau on Riverside Drive. La Guardia is reliably reported to have taken one look at the place and exploded, "What! *Me* in *that?*" and opted for the old wooden house facing the East River. Laguardia prided himself on being a simple man.

A description of the East Side's more interesting points can never be as good as an actual visit there. A stroll down one of the side streets between Fifth and Madison Avenue, hot chestnuts and pretzels from a street vendor or a horse drawn ride through Central Park are all sensory experiences filled with discoveries that words cannot cover. The people who live on the East Side like the relative quiet of it so close to the innumerable delicatessens and antique shops that give it flavor.

At one time or another, though, they all do the same thing. They go down to one of the dead-end streets facing out over the East River and stare down at its swirling currents. Sometimes they stand there for a few minutes, just long enough to refresh themselves. Other times they stand there for hours on end, feeling the current of water against the sense of New York City behind them.

Missing from that half of Manhattan bordered by the Hudson River, Central Park West and Fifty-Ninth Street are the Neo Palaces and studied elegance of the East. Diversity has always characterized this area. Its residential development was slower than that of the East Side so its neighborhoods, streets and avenues grew into a diffuse variety that dazzles the imagination as the kaleidoscope dazzles the eyes with constantly shifting patterns.

The West Side's haphazard growth is the result of settlement by many of the immigrants from the Lower East Side whose improved status impelled them to seek out identities of their own far from the older more established neighborhoods of the East Side

One vivid example of this was the nineteenth century collision between the wealthy members of both groups over who represented the real "Society." The old Academy of Music on East Fourteenth Street had always been run by descendants of English and Dutch families with names like Van Rensselaer or Morris. These people considered—with some justification—the mid-nineteenth-century robber barons, the Morgans, the Rockefellers, Goulds and Vanderbilts as vulgar *nouveau riche*; unrefined railroad tycoons and oil moguls, all unsavory in habit and

Amidst the towering steel, concrete and glass all around, one can still pause for a moment's thought —or step back in time...

70

deportment and not fit to adorn the balcony boxes of true culture at the Academy of Music.

Snubbed by the old money, with no place to show off their diamond stickpins and wive's jewelry, the 'New Society' erected the Metropolitan Opera House on West Thirty-Ninth Street and sectioned off tiers with names like the Golden and Diamond Horseshoe where they could see each other to best advantage. Not surprisingly the old Metropolitan Opera House was never noted for its acoustics.

What the West Side has instead of all this is color and tremendous excitement of a type found nowhere else. On Eighth Avenue and Thirty-Second Street is a strip of Greek-Turkish-Middle Eastern night spots where the *mezrachi* antipasto is seasoned with bouzoukee music and belly dancing. Ninth Avenue from Thirty-Seventh to Forty-Third Streets has one of the world's best open food markets. Seventh Avenue and the garment district are devoted to fashion and the manufacture of clothing, New York's largest manufacturing enterprise (printing and publishing are second.) The visitor will certainly enjoy the Diamond District with its jewelry stores and diamond cutting shops along Sixth Avenue and the Forties. During Prohibition, the West Fifties were known as the wettest streets in America.

Above all there is Broadway, the one avenue that crystallized this diversity into its own form. If Fifth Avenue is Manhattan's spine, then Broadway is its heartbeat.

Broadway has always been lively. The southern end of this Indian hunting trail blossomed into an area of churches and elegant neighborhoods similar to those on Fifth Avenue but, by the 1870s as it pushed its way above Thirty-Fourth Street, its saloons, gambling houses and theaters were drawing in a different crowd. By 1882, the Theater strip running from Fourteenth to Forty-Second Street nicknamed the "Rialto," rivalled the activity of Madison and Union Squares. By then, Broadway was siphoning off the "slave market," the teams of unemployed actors who swarmed around Union Square looking for summer work.

By World War One, the transformation was com-

Left-hand page: construction under way. This page: one of the numerous French restaurants in New York, and one of the city's (rare) open-air cafés.

plete. Vaudeville music halls where Al Jolson sang lined the sidewalks. The producer George M. Cohan who claimed to have more musical productions running simultaneously than anyone in the world was to have a statue of himself erected near Times Square. Times Square itself (named after the New York Times Building) was crisscrossed with trolley tracks.

On Central Park West and 77th Street at the precise latitude of the Metropolitan Museum of Art stands the West Side's answer to the East's cultural challenge: the American Museum of Natural His-

tory. Founded within a year after the Met with a modest collection of stuffed birds and mammals from a German naturalist's collection, it has grown into an extraordinarily rich collection of animal life, jewelry and astronomy exhibits, housed in 58 halls. The Museum of Natural History grew in the exciting days of Darwin, Pasteur and Lister when worlds within worlds were opening their secrets to nineteenth century intellects. The seventeen separate units include the Hayden Planetarium, built in 1935, which includes a mechanical depiction of the solar system. The gem collection was the object of one of

the most spectacular thefts in the annals of crime. The 563-carat sapphire *Star of India* was lifted one night by a group of acrobatic thieves inspired by a movie and was not recovered until much later.

The motion picture *West Side Story,* an updated musical version of Romeo and Juliet, was filmed in a neighborhood of crowded tenements and narrow streets that no longer exists. On the spot where youth gangs of the 1950's fought each other in the film stands the crown jewel of the West Side and possibly the city: Lincoln Center for the Performing Arts, at Broadway and 64th Street. Lincoln Center's

On these two pages, some curious or unexpected scenes, near the East River.

five-building complex houses nearly every type of musical, theatrical or dance enterprise devised by the western imagination. The Center also includes an outdoor amphitheater, museum, library and the Julliard School of Music. The Metropolitan Opera and New York Philharmonic Hall caused lively controversy when they moved to Lincoln Center in the 1960's from their original locations.

Despite a storm of public protest, the Old Met, with its horseshoe tiers, was torn down. Carnegie Hall, the original home of the New York Philharmonic, was narrowly saved from a similar fate.

Lincoln Center was not the first threat to this venerable house's existence. Carnegie Hall on West Fifty-Seventh Street and Seventh Avenue has had an existence resembling that of a silent movie heroine who is always saved at the last instant from train wheels, dynamite blasts and wrecking balls. This neo-Italianate rock pile with its heavy offset tower and immense charm was erected in 1891 through the efforts of an Oratorio Society looking for its own concert hall. It was financed by Andrew Carnegie, Scottish philanthropist and steel-maker. Tchaikovsky opened the hall in May of that year

78

playing his own compositions. Carnegie, whose own tastes seem to have run to bagpipe music, tired of supporting the hall with his own money and a hastily organized subscription saved it. In 1925 a syndicate purchased the hall, saving it from another financial disaster, and it continued to present artists ranging from Benny Goodman to Toscanini to the Rolling Stones, all of whom have praised its outstanding acoustics (which were not one of the Old Met's qualities). In 1960 demolition was threatened again. It was feared the hall would compete with Philharmonic Hall at Lincoln Center, into which the orchestra was moving. New York City won a court fight to save it, purchased it and kept it in business. Today both Carnegie and Philharmonic Hall play to full houses without damaging each other.

La Belle Epoque, the last half of the nineteenth century and the beginning of the twentieth, is seen, rather inaccurately, as a long unbroken period of peace and growing affluence. The fact is New York City, America and Europe swung back and forth like a pendulum between great wealth and social ferment, their catalytic economies plagued by sudden, savage recessions. Their names read like a roster of military defeats; Reconstruction (which followed the Civil War), the *Crédit Mobilier* scandal (a collapsing railroad bubble in which millions of dollars were lost), the Panics of 1890 and 1904, and the Depression.

During these periods, Harlem, the northern tier of Manhattan, experienced raised and dashed hopes, growth and collapse in steady cadence, until the Great Depression of the 1930's finished off its chances of becoming a middle-class neighborhood. A superb group of neo-Georgian and Italian Renaissance houses were built at St Nicholas Place and priced for middle income owners just in time for the Panic of 1904, which forced their sale, at a huge loss, to their builders.

In 1925 John D. Rockefeller attempted an experiment in low income housing which would be more tasteful and pleasant than the tenements and crowded streets which characterized the area. The Dunbar Apartment complex was a combination garden-courtyard group of buildings done in Spanish Renaissance; however, it failed as a cooperative af-

ter the Great Depression hit, proving too expensive for the really poor. The concept of cooperative low and middle income housing was not to appear again until after World War Two. By that time, the depression had done its work. Harlem and the city teemed with the poor, the desperate and the hungry who had come to New York looking for work. Harlem's unique vitality, its jazz clubs and Negro consciousness would co-exist with urban poverty.

On West 160th Street at the highest point in Manhattan stands a white wooden Georgian mansion, once the country house of a Colonel Roger Morris. This house served as George Washington's headquarters after his defeat in the battle of Long Island and was purchased in 1810 by a French merchant named Stephen Jumel. The house is in a perfect state of preservation.

Jumel's widow married Aaron Burr, a former Vice President then in his late seventies and one of the more bizarre American historical figures, who, after mortally wounding Alexander Hamilton in a duel, seemed to have embarked on a series of conspiracies whose purposes were obscure even then. Burr's wife survived his death and became a complete eccentric. Legend has it she moved to Paris for a few years where she used to stand up in her carriage and command the Parisians to "make way for the widow of the Vice President of the United States." She died in the handsome house after three years, a total recluse. The name of the area on which the Morris-Jumel mansion stands was changed from Harlem Heights to Washington Heights.

Even farther north than this outpost of Colonial times, at Fort Tryon Park and 166th Street, there stands an anachronism so startling in the New World that its existence can hardly be credited. The Clois-

Top left: some of the stately buildings situated along Central Park West. Top right: the Dakota Building. Bottom: a cross-town canyon seen from the West Side. An avenue at the beginning of Harlem.

ters is technically a museum of medieval European art replete with tapestries and sarcophagi from the Middle Ages. The separate units comprising it, the chapel and arches, were imported stone by stone from various parts of Europe, mostly Southern France and rebuilt to the last detail in New York City.

The Cloisters is New York's most visible proof of the often invisible bonds connecting it with its origins across the Atlantic.

Greater New York was formed in 1898 with the addition of the City of Brooklyn and The Bronx. Latest census figures place its population at eleven million as a whole, of which the borough of Manhattan is the

On these two pages: various views of the black area of Harlem. Harlem resembles Chinatown in the sense that it is a city within the city.

most densely populated.

The Bronx is the only one of New York's boroughs actually connected to the United States mainland and the only one prefixed with "The." This curious name derives from a Danish Lutheran immigrant named Jonas Bronck who purchased five hundred acres of land between the Harlem and what was later called The Bronx river. The whole area was known as The Bronck's Farm, and the name stuck long after the farm had disappeared. Forty-two square miles in size, The Bronx is most famous for its Botanical Gardens and one of the most beautiful open zoos in the world.

Next to Manhattan, *Brooklyn* is the most famous of Greater New York's boroughs. In Dutch times it was a flat stretch of land covered with cranberry bogs and peach groves. The borough itself is the end product of mergers between numerous small vil-

Houses and views of Harlem. We are now far uptown, at 160th St.

Some curious views of the big city. Facing: Jumel Mansion, which was George Washington's headquarters during one of the battles of the War of Independence; the room and the table which he used as his office.

Above: The Cloisters, seen from Fort Tryon Park. On the left of the photo, the majestic expanse of the Hudson. Following pages: the Brooklyn and Manhattan Bridges, seen from the Wall Street area.

Left and right: historic Brooklyn Bridge. Below: Queensborough Bridge.

Top right: this striking view of Brooklyn was taken from the East River, with Manhattan Bridge in the foreground. Bottom: Brooklyn Bridge by night.

lages that coalesced into the City of Brooklyn and later combined with New York. Brooklyn has always had an ambivalent relationship with its partner across the East River. Some of its neighborhoods, such as Brooklyn Heights and Flatbush, are as beautiful as any to be found in Manhattan; the Brooklyn Museum rivals the Metropolitan, and were it not a part of New York, Brooklyn's population of two and a half million would make it the fourth biggest city in the United States.

In area, *Queens* is the largest section of New York and the exact process of its development is rather obscure. We know the Dutch chartered the settle-

ments of Maspeth, Middleburg and Flushing (a corruption of the Dutch town *Vlissengen*) in the early 1640s and allowed English settlers to live there before the Anglo-Dutch war lost the whole of New Netherlands to Britain. Its name comes from Queen's County, a name given to it by the British in honor of Catherine of Braganza, Charles II's Queen. Unlike Brooklyn, Queen's spotty sections did not grow together until the end of World War One and there is a lack of a single tradition to give it a distinct identity. Post-World War Two housing developments built up the population and ended its last trace of rural sections. Today it is laced with a staggering network of highways and throughways. It is the site of LaGuardia and Kennedy airports and its Great Jamaica Bay is a wildlife refuge inhabited by migratory and native birds.

Five miles out in Upper New York Bay lies Staten Island, nestled less than a quarter of a mile from the

Top: general view of Brooklyn. Left, above and right: views of the Bronx.

coast of New Jersey. Curiosities abound in this little place. Todt Hill in its center is not only the highest point on the island, it is the highest point on the entire Eastern seaboard from Maine to Florida. It is famous as the turn-around point of the Staten Island ferry ride, the greatest and cheapest way to spend an afternoon in the city. It was named Staten Eylant by the Dutch after the States General of the Netherlands, yet its capital is Richmond, a British name. The Historical Society of Staten Island has preserved Richmondtown and restored it as an authentic seventeenth and eighteenth century village.

Staten Island was involved for a long time in various tugs-of-war between claimants. The Dutch possession of it was punctuated by numerous Indian wars. The New Jersey Lords, Berkeley and Carteret, repeatedly claimed it as their own but an 1833 joint commission passed it to New York. Today the island has numerous small communities and it is connected to the city by the longest suspension bridge in the world, the Verrazano-Narrows bridge.

Among the numerous old houses and landmarks on Staten Island is one in Rosebank in which Giuseppe Garibaldi, the Italian liberator, lived for a year and a half after the collapse of the Roman Republic. He and a friend lived in poverty in a back room making and selling candles before returning to Italy and leading the March of the One Thousand that freed Sicily and Naples.

We thus conclude on a "European" note. But New York will always remain one of the great symbols of the United States.

Above: the arrivals hall at Kennedy Airport. Right: assorted views of Coney Island and its world-famous Luna Park. Following pages: view of Long Island; the Statue of Liberty; the Manhattan skyline seen from Queens cemetery; Jamaica Bay, where nature still remains more or less intact.

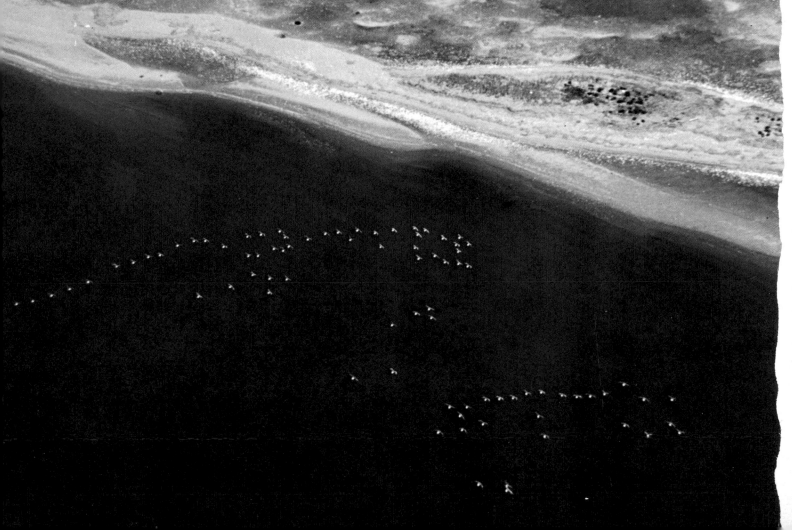